Oklahoma
Sooners
TRIVIA CHALLENGE

SOURCEBOOKS, INC.
NAPERVILLE, ILLINOIS

Copyright © 2008 by Sourcebooks, Inc.
Cover and internal design © 2008 by Sourcebooks, Inc.
Cover images © AP Images

All rights reserved. No part of this book may be reproduced in any form or by any electronic or mechanical means including information storage and retrieval systems—except in the case of brief quotations embodied in critical articles or reviews—without permission in writing from its publisher, Sourcebooks, Inc.

All brand names and product names used in this book are trademarks, registered trademarks, or trade names of their respective holders. Sourcebooks, Inc., is not associated with any product or vendor in this book.

Published by Sourcebooks, Inc.
P.O. Box 4410, Naperville, Illinois 60567-4410
(630) 961-3900
Fax: (630) 961-2168
www.sourcebooks.com

Printed and bound in Canada
WC 10 9 8 7 6 5 4 3 2 1

Oklahoma has won more national championships, had more Heisman Trophy winners, and produced more All-Americans than just about any program in the nation. The school's distinctions fill the NCAA record book and its players' names line the college, pro, and myriad other Halls of Fame. Oklahoma boasts multiple legendary coaches—from Bennie Owen to Bob Stoops—and the players in between have given Sooner football buffs as many colorful moments as statistical milestones.

These 200 questions should test your knowledge of both, from all-time passing records to once-in-a-lifetime game-winning plays. From the quirky comments famous coaches have made to the game-day traditions cooked up by the crowd. If you're both a stat geek and a passionate fan, you should be able to get to the last page without clicking on your browser or calling a classmate. The questions and topics are designed to grow tougher, taking you from the big records and names to the obscure and bizarre. Get half of the answers right, and Bennie Owen would probably still be proud. (Just don't miss the one about which Sooner facility today bears his name.) Anything less than 50 percent, and you'll risk the long Oklahoma tradition of winning records.

THE BOB STOOPS ERA

1. **Oklahoma won a national championship in Bob Stoops's _____ year as head coach.**

    a. 1st
    b. 2nd
    c. 3rd
    d. 4th

2. **Who did the Sooners defeat that year in the Orange Bowl to clinch the national title?**

    a. Texas
    b. USC
    c. Miami
    d. Florida State

3. **Oklahoma had a perfect record that season, improving the Sooners' mark from what record the previous year?**

    a. 9–3
    b. 8–4
    c. 7–5
    d. 6–6

4. **Stoops was hired at Oklahoma from what job?**

    a. head coach at Florida
    b. defensive coordinator at Florida
    c. head coach at Iowa
    d. defensive coordinator at Kansas State

5. **Bob Stoops is one of the _____ active coaches in Div. I football.**

   a. youngest
   b. oldest
   c. highest-paid
   d. longest-tenured

6. **Oklahoma played in the January 2, 2008, Cotton Bowl against which team?**

   a. Virginia
   b. West Virginia
   c. Virginia Tech
   d. Maryland

7. **What was the Sooners' record the season before Bob Stoops arrived?**

   a. 7–4
   b. 6–5
   c. 5–6
   d. 4–7

8. **From 2000 to 2006, only one team in Div. I football had a higher winning percentage than Oklahoma. What team was it?**

   a. Florida
   b. USC
   c. Texas
   d. Boise State

9. **Who led the Sooners in rushing in 2007?**

   a. Allen Patrick
   b. DeMarco Murray
   c. Chris Brown
   d. Mossis Madu

10. Who led the Sooners in receiving, with total yards and receptions?

a. Jermaine Gresham
b. Malcolm Kelly
c. Manuel Johnson
d. Juaquin Iglesias

11. In 2007, Oklahoma went undefeated _____.

a. the entire season
b. at home
c. on the road
d. against Texas, Texas A&M, and Texas Tech

12. Stoops was a four-year starter at defensive back for what program?

a. Oklahoma
b. Nebraska
c. Iowa State
d. Iowa

13. Which two former quarterbacks are on the 2008 coaching staff?

a. Jason White and Josh Heupel
b. Cale Gundy and Josh Heupel
c. Jamelle Holieway and Cale Gundy
d. Nate Hybl and Jamelle Holieway

14. Bob Stoops's younger brother, Mike Stoops, became head coach of what program?

a. Washington
b. Washington State
c. Arizona
d. Arizona State

15. Which other Div. I head coach was NOT previously an assistant to Bob Stoops?

a. Nebraska's Bob Pelini
b. Texas Tech's Mike Leach
c. Kansas's Mark Mangino
d. Texas A&M's Mike Sherman

16. **How many yards did Adrian Peterson rush for as a freshman?**

    a. 980
    b. 1,118
    c. 1,648
    d. 1,925

17. **That was a _____ freshman record.**

    a. Sooner
    b. Big 12
    c. NCAA
    d. all of the above

18. **How many times that season did Peterson rush for at least 100 yards, an NCAA record?**

    a. 7
    b. 9
    c. 11
    d. 13

19. **In a 2003 game against UCLA, which Sooner scored three touchdowns, all on punt returns?**

    a. Antonio Perkins
    b. Donte Nicholson
    c. Jejuan Rankins
    d. Mark Clayton

20. **Before Bob Stoops became the head coach in 1999, Oklahoma had NOT produced a consensus All-American since which year?**

    a. 1992
    b. 1988
    c. 1980
    d. 1976

21. **In 1999, Bob Stoops became the _____ coach in Oklahoma history.**

    a. 8th
    b. 14th
    c. 21st
    d. 28th

TRADITIONS

22. What are Oklahoma's school colors?
   a. scarlet and cream
   b. crimson and cream
   c. garnet and cream
   d. red and white

23. What is the Sooner Schooner?
   a. a covered wagon
   b. a caboose
   c. an Indian chief
   d. a steamboat

24. What are the names of the two white ponies that help make up the mascot?
   a. Okla and Homa
   b. Bonnie and Clyde
   c. Bennie and Bud
   d. Boomer and Sooner

25. What does the name "Sooner" refer to?
   a. the first family that settled the Oklahoma Territory in 1889
   b. the Choctow Indian word for "settler"
   c. a particularly powerful class of tornadoes
   d. settlers who left for the Oklahoma Territory sooner than they were supposed to

26. According to the Oklahoma chant, "thousands strong join heart and song _____."

a. in cheering on the Sooners
b. in beating down Nebraska
c. in alma mater's praise
d. in defending Oklahoma

27. The football team was first called the Sooners in which year?

a. 1900
b. 1908
c. 1915
d. 1923

28. The Sooners were previously known by what two other nicknames?

a. the Settlers and the Oklahomans
b. the Rough Riders and the Boomers
c. the Cowboys and the Buffaloes
d. the Indians and the Shooters

29. Oklahoma's fight song was originally created in 1905 by combining and improvising which fight songs from two other universities?

a. Yale's "Boola Boola" and North Carolina's "I'm a Tarheel Born"
b. Harvard's "Fight Fiercely, Harvard" and Duke's "Fight! Blue Devils, Fight!"
c. Nebraska's "There's No Place Like Nebraska" and Michigan's "The Victors"
d. Ohio State's "Buckeye Battle Cry" and Illinois' "Oskee Wow Wow"

NATIONAL CHAMPIONSHIPS

30. Entering the 2008 season, how many national championships has Oklahoma won?

   a. 3
   b. 5
   c. 7
   d. 9

31. Oklahoma won the national championship in 2000 after _____ the previous season.

   a. being unranked
   b. being under probation
   c. having a losing record
   d. changing coaches

32. Going into the 2008 season, only one program has won more Associated Press National Championships than Oklahoma. Which program is it?

   a. Nebraska
   b. Alabama
   c. USC
   d. Notre Dame

33. Oklahoma twice won back-to-back national championships in what years?

   a. 1950–1951 and 1975–1976
   b. 1949–1950 and 1985–1986
   c. 1973–1974 and 1985–1986
   d. 1955–1956 and 1974–1975

34. Which program has Oklahoma NOT defeated in a bowl game to win a national championship?

a. Kentucky
b. Maryland
c. Penn State
d. Alabama

35. Which year did Oklahoma win its first national championship?

a. 1932
b. 1941
c. 1950
d. 1956

36. Oklahoma won its first national title under which coach?

a. Bennie Owen
b. Tom Stidham
c. Bud Wilkinson
d. Barry Switzer

37. How many of Oklahoma's national championships followed perfect seasons?

a. 3
b. 4
c. 5
d. 6

38. How many times was Oklahoma also a wire-to-wire No. 1 team in the AP weekly poll?

a. 0
b. 1
c. 2
d. 3

39. How many times has Oklahoma been the AP's preseason favorite and also gone on to win the national championship? (The preseason poll began in 1950.)

   a. 0
   b. 2
   c. 4
   d. 6

40. The Sooners have also been recognized by different polls over the years with several national championships that the university doesn't consider official. Including the titles voted on by the Associated Press, how many Oklahoma teams have been selected national champion by at least one of the voting bodies?

   a. 7
   b. 10
   c. 12
   d. 16

41. Oklahoma won its first Associated Press national championship despite _____.

   a. losing twice that year to Nebraska
   b. winning only nine games
   c. losing to Kentucky in the Sugar Bowl
   d. playing eight games on the road

42. Oklahoma was recognized with national championships in 1956 and 1974 _____.

   a. by beating Michigan
   b. without playing in a bowl game
   c. after winning 12 games
   d. after winning the Rose Bowl

43. Oklahoma won the 1975 national championship thanks to what upset that year in the Rose Bowl?

   a. Texas beat Notre Dame
   b. Arizona State beat Nebraska
   c. UCLA beat Ohio State
   d. Alabama beat Penn State

OKLAHOMA MEMORIAL

44. In the park just east of Oklahoma Memorial Stadium, a series of statues commemorate which Sooner legends?

a. the teams that won national championships
b. the coaches that lead OU to national titles
c. the school's Heisman Trophy winners
d. the first four coaches in the program's history

45. In 2008, what is the playing surface inside the stadium?

a. artificial turf
b. natural grass
c. natural grass on the playing field and artificial turf on the sidelines
d. Indiangrass, the Oklahoma state grass

46. Oklahoma Memorial Stadium was originally named to honor the university personnel who had died during which war?

a. the Spanish-American War
b. the Civil War
c. World War I
d. World War II

47. The field inside Memorial Stadium is named in whose honor?

   a. Oklahoma's first Heisman Trophy winner, Steve Owens
   b. former Oklahoma coach, Bennie Owen
   c. former university president, William Owen
   d. Oklahoma Senator Robert Owen

48. When was the stadium renamed Gaylord Family-Oklahoma Memorial Stadium?

   a. 1974
   b. 1989
   c. 1994
   d. 2002

49. Who are the Gaylords?

   a. publishers of *The Oklahoman* newspaper
   b. founders of Oklahoma University
   c. the state's most powerful political dynasty
   d. owners of the state's largest oil refinery

50. Which year did the Sooners play their first game at the site of Oklahoma Memorial Stadium?

   a. 1910
   b. 1923
   c. 1935
   d. 1947

51. In 1925, the university originally intended to build a football stadium that would share space and also serve as what other campus amenity?

   a. the health center
   b. the psychology department
   c. the admissions office
   d. the student union

52. Up until 1949, what was the capacity of Oklahoma Memorial Stadium?

a. 25,000
b. 32,000
c. 44,000
d. 50,000

53. What is Oklahoma's longest winning streak at the home stadium?

a. 15 games
b. 25 games
c. 32 games
d. 47 games

QUARTERBACKS

54. Jason White became the Sooners' _____ Heisman Trophy-winner in 2003.

   a. 1st
   b. 2nd
   c. 3rd
   d. 4th

55. Jason White was a finalist for the Heisman Trophy two years in a row. The second year (after winning the trophy in 2003), where did he finish in the voting?

   a. 2nd
   b. 3rd
   c. 4th
   d. 5th

56. White was joined among the Heisman finalists in 2004 by which Oklahoma teammate?

   a. Kejuan Jones
   b. Brandon Jones
   c. Mark Clayton
   d. Adrian Peterson

57. Past Heisman Trophy-winners are given a permanent vote for the award. After winning it himself in 2003 and being a finalist in 2004, who did White say he voted for in 2004?

   a. himself
   b. Matt Leinart
   c. Adrian Peterson
   d. Alex Smith

58. Jason White left Oklahoma as _____.

   a. a junior
   b. a senior
   c. a fifth-year senior
   d. a sixth-year senior

59. Jamelle Holieway led the Sooners to the 1985 national championship while he was _____.

   a. a freshman
   b. a sophomore
   c. a junior
   d. a senior

60. Who did Josh Heupel lose the 2000 Heisman Trophy to?

   a. Drew Brees
   b. Chris Weinke
   c. LaDanian Tomlinson
   d. Michael Vick

61. Jason White suffered which major injury two different times during his Oklahoma career?

   a. rotator-cuff tear
   b. ACL tear
   c. broken wrist
   d. slipped disc

62. Which future star quarterback transferred from Oklahoma to UCLA after breaking his ankle and being replaced in the starting lineup?

   a. Cade McNown
   b. Troy Aikman
   c. Carson Palmer
   d. Joe Montana

63. Which player set a Sooner record with total offense in a single season, with 3,773 yards?

   a. Jason White
   b. Sam Bradford
   c. Paul Thompson
   d. Josh Heupel

64. Who holds the record for total offense in a career?

   a. Jason White
   b. Josh Heupel
   c. Cale Gundy
   d. Jamelle Holieway

65. How many touchdown passes did Jason White throw in his career?

   a. 41
   b. 50
   c. 72
   d. 81

66. Josh Heupel had how many consecutive 300-yard passing games in 1999 and then again in 2000?

   a. 2
   b. 3
   c. 4
   d. 5

67. From 1999 to 2000, Josh Heupel went _____ consecutive games with at least one touchdown pass.

   a. 8
   b. 12
   c. 19
   d. 25

68. Jason White won which award in both 2003 and 2004?

a. the Heisman Trophy
b. the Johnny Unitas Award
c. the Davey O'Brien Award
d. the Maxwell Award

69. Which award did Jason White never win?

a. the Heisman Trophy for player of the year
b. the Davey O'Brien for outstanding quarterback
c. the Maxwell Award for player of the year
d. the Walter Camp Trophy for player of the year

70. Which Oklahoma quarterback completed 25 of 31 passes for 329 yards and two touchdowns in the 1991 Gator Bowl?

a. Cale Gundy
b. Jamelle Holieway
c. Terence Brown
d. Garrick McGee

71. In 2003, Jason White set an Oklahoma record for touchdown passes in a single season with how many?

a. 28
b. 35
c. 40
d. 50

72. Which quarterback was NOT among the Heisman Trophy vote-getters edged out by Oklahoma's Jason White in 2003?

a. Eli Manning
b. Matt Leinart
c. Vince Young
d. Ben Rothlisberger

CONFERENCE PLAY

73. The Big 12 formed by combining the Big Eight with four Texas schools from which disbanding conference?
   a. the Southwest Conference
   b. the Southern Conference
   c. the Texas League
   d. the Gulf Coast Conference

74. The Big 12 is divided today into which two divisions?
   a. the Eastern and Western
   b. the Northern and Southern
   c. the Plains and Gulf
   d. the Charter and the Expansion

75. Which school is NOT in Oklahoma's division?
   a. Oklahoma State
   b. Kansas State
   c. Baylor
   d. Texas Tech

76. Between 2000 and 2007, how many Big 12 conference titles did the Sooners win?
   a. 4
   b. 5
   c. 6
   d. 7

77. Which conference opponent spoiled Oklahoma's perfect 2003 season and 14 straight weeks at No. 1 in the Big 12 Championship Game?

   a. Kansas
   b. Kansas State
   c. Nebraska
   d. Texas

78. Which is the first conference Oklahoma ever joined?

   a. the Southwest Conference
   b. the Great Plains Conference
   c. the Missouri Valley Conference
   d. the Big Six Conference

79. Which conference was NOT one of the predecessors of the Big 12?

   a. the Big Ten
   b. the Big Eight
   c. the Big Seven
   d. the Big Six

80. Which year did competition in the new Big 12 begin?

   a. 2000
   b. 1998
   c. 1996
   d. 1990

81. Where is the Big 12 headquartered?

   a. Norman, Oklahoma
   b. Lincoln, Nebraska
   c. Dallas, Texas
   d. Irving, Texas

82. **The Big 12 covers schools from how many different states?**

    a. 4
    b. 5
    c. 7
    d. 8

83. **Starting in 1973, Oklahoma finished the season either first or second in the Big Eight for how many consecutive seasons?**

    a. 10
    b. 16
    c. 20
    d. 24

84. **The Oklahoma–Kansas series—one of the longest uninterrupted matchups in college football—began in which year?**

    a. 1899
    b. 1903
    c. 1910
    d. 1919

85. **Starting in 1937, Oklahoma won how many consecutive games over Kansas State?**

    a. 24
    b. 32
    c. 45
    d. 60

BENNIE, BUD, AND BARRY

86. Barry Switzer is one of the only coaches in history to _____.

   a. win a college national championship and a Super Bowl
   b. coach three different schools to a national championship
   c. return to college coaching after winning a Super Bowl
   d. resign after winning a national championship

87. What school did Switzer play for?

   a. Oklahoma
   b. Alabama
   c. Arkansas
   d. Iowa

88. Which NFL team did Barry Switzer coach?

   a. the Dallas Cowboys
   b. the Miami Dolphins
   c. the Oakland Raiders
   d. the New England Patriots

89. Why did Switzer resign from Oklahoma after the 1988 season?

   a. to run for political office
   b. to accept a coaching job in the NFL
   c. because of illness
   d. because of NCAA probation

90. Coach Barry Switzer won _____ at Oklahoma.

   a. a national championship in his first season
   b. two national championships in his first three seasons
   c. three straight national championships
   d. a national championship in his final season

91. Barry Switzer referred to what game as "the most disappointing loss of my career"?

a. Arkansas's 31–6 upset in the 1976 Orange Bowl
b. Oklahoma's 35–31 regular-season loss to Nebraska in 1971
c. Oklahoma's 20–14 loss to Miami in the 1988 Orange Bowl
d. Oklahoma's 13–6 Citrus Bowl loss to Clemson in Switzer's final game in 1989

92. What was Bud Wilkinson's real first name?

a. William
b. Charles
c. David
d. Jerome

93. Wilkinson won three straight national championships as a player for what program?

a. Minnesota
b. Michigan
c. Ohio State
d. Penn State

94. How old was Wilkinson when he became head coach at Oklahoma?

a. 24
b. 31
c. 36
d. 40

95. Wilkinson is often credited with inventing what offensive scheme?

a. the spread
b. the no-huddle
c. the wing-T
d. the wishbone

96. How many losing seasons did Bud Wilkinson have in 17 years at Oklahoma?

a. 0
b. 1
c. 3
d. 5

97. After he retired from coaching at Oklahoma, Wilkinson ran for what political seat?

a. mayor of Norman
b. governor of Oklahoma
c. U.S. senator
d. president

98. After retiring, Wilkinson later revived his coaching career by taking what job?

a. head coach at Oklahoma a second time
b. head coach at Nebraska
c. head coach of the Chicago Bears
d. head coach of the St. Louis Cardinals

99. Wilkinson also had a career later in life as a _____.

a. restaurant owner
b. television analyst
c. English professor
d. university president

100. After 1907, Bennie Owen coached without _____.

a. his right arm
b. his left leg
c. eyesight
d. hearing

101. Owen also served what other role at Oklahoma?

a. track coach
b. president
c. basketball coach
d. trustee

102. Owen became a member of the first class of the _____.

a. Oklahoma Hall of Fame
b. Pro Football Hall of Fame
c. College Football Hall of Fame
d. Oklahoma medical school

HISTORY

103. Which year did Oklahoma play its first football game?

   a. 1890
   b. 1895
   c. 1900
   d. 1910

104. The November 8, 1952, game vs. Notre Dame was Oklahoma's first _____.

   a. night game
   b. home game in Memorial Stadium
   c. televised game
   d. integrated game

105. Who was Oklahoma's first football coach?

   a. John Harris
   b. Vernon Parrington
   c. Mark McMahon
   d. Bennie Owen

106. What was the team's record that year?

   a. 5–0
   b. 3–3–1
   c. 2–4
   d. 0–1

107. In its second season, the Oklahoma football team played without _____.

   a. uniforms
   b. a coach
   c. opponents
   d. a football

108. The football program at Oklahoma started before _____.

   a. the university was fully established
   b. the game was played at any other college
   c. Oklahoma became a state
   d. the town of Norman was settled

109. Which year did Oklahoma beat Texas for the first time?

   a. 1905
   b. 1915
   c. 1925
   d. 1930

110. Who was the first African-American football player at Oklahoma?

   a. Prentice Gautt
   b. Gale Sayers
   c. Billy Sims
   d. Bob Gibson

111. The Big 12 named what conference honor after that player?

   a. its athlete of the year award
   b. its championship MVP trophy
   c. its postgraduate scholarships
   d. its sportsmanship award

112. During the 1970 season, the Sooners switched to which offensive scheme, which was to become one of their trademarks?

a. the spread
b. the no-huddle
c. the West Coast offense
d. the wishbone

113. When the Sooners were placed on probation in 1988, they were banned for two years from _____.

a. traveling to road games and signing new recruits
b. playing on television and in bowl games
c. signing a shoe contract and earning merchandise proceeds
d. setting and competing for NCAA records

BIG GAMES AND BOWLS

114. Oklahoma lost the 2004 Sugar Bowl and national championship to which team?

a. Texas
b. USC
c. Florida
d. LSU

115. Who did the Sooners lose the 2005 Orange Bowl and national championship to?

a. Texas
b. USC
c. Florida
d. LSU

116. Boise State won the 2007 Fiesta Bowl over Oklahoma, 43–42, with what play in overtime?

a. a hook-and-lateral play for a 50-yard touchdown and extra point
b. a fumblerooski and two-point conversion
c. a touchdown pass from wide receiver Vinny Perretta and a trick two-point conversion
d. a fake field goal followed by a trick two-point conversion

117. Boise State and Oklahoma combined to score how many points in the final 1 minute, 26 seconds in regulation of that game?

a. 14
b. 18
c. 22
d. 28

118. **Oklahoma went how many straight seasons in the 1990s without a bowl bid?**

    a. 2
    b. 3
    c. 4
    d. 5

119. **Oklahoma and USC were paired in the 2004 BCS title game to the exclusion of what other undefeated team from the SEC?**

    a. Tennessee
    b. Alabama
    c. LSU
    d. Auburn

120. **Oklahoma has played in which bowl game more times than any other?**

    a. the Rose Bowl
    b. the Cotton Bowl
    c. the Orange Bowl
    d. the Sugar Bowl

121. **Which bowl game has Oklahoma never played in?**

    a. the Bluebonnet Bowl
    b. the Holiday Bowl
    c. the Hancock Bowl
    d. the Freedom Bowl

122. **As of the 2008 season, Oklahoma was last shutout in which bowl game?**

    a. the 1994 Copper Bowl against BYU
    b. the 1989 Citrus Bowl against Clemson
    c. the 1978 Orange Bowl against Arkansas
    d. the 1963 Orange Bowl against Alabama

123. **In a 1986 game with Kansas, Oklahoma set a school defensive record by allowing the Jayhawks how many yards rushing?**

    a. 1 yard
    b. 0 yards
    c. –10 yards
    d. –52 yards

124. **From 1963 to 2005, Oklahoma played in seven different games matching the No. 1 and No. 2 teams in the poll. How many of those meetings did Oklahoma win?**

    a. 1
    b. 3
    c. 5
    d. 7

125. **Which year did the Sooners make their first trip to the Rose Bowl?**

    a. 1941
    b. 1968
    c. 1984
    d. 2003

126. **This decade, Oklahoma became one of _____ schools in college football to win the Orange, Sugar, Rose, Fiesta, and Cotton bowls.**

    a. 2
    b. 4
    c. 5
    d. 8

127. **During the 41–7 victory over Wyoming in the 1976 Fiesta Bowl, the Sooners did NOT _____ once during the entire game.**

    a. kick a field goal
    b. punt
    c. give up possession
    d. go for an extra point

128. Oklahoma avenged a loss to which regular-season opponent with a victory in the 1979 Orange Bowl rematch?

a. Colorado
b. Nebraska
c. Texas
d. Notre Dame

129. The "Game of the Century" refers to which Oklahoma matchup?

a. the 1971 regular-season game with Nebraska
b. the January 1, 1972, Sugar Bowl game against Auburn
c. the 1976 regular-season game with Nebraska
d. the January 1, 1976, Orange Bowl against Michigan

130. In 1971, which three Big Eight teams finished first, second, and third in the final polls?

a. Nebraska, Oklahoma, and Colorado
b. Oklahoma, Iowa State, and Oklahoma State
c. Oklahoma, Colorado, and Texas
d. Nebraska, Oklahoma, and Kansas

131. During the 1978 season, Oklahoma avenged a regular-season loss to what team with a victory in the Orange Bowl?

a. Texas
b. Nebraska
c. Oklahoma State
d. Texas A&M

132. What was the first bowl game Oklahoma ever played in?

a. the 1928 Rose Bowl
b. the 1939 Orange Bowl
c. the 1947 Gator Bowl
d. the 1949 Sugar Bowl

133. During the 1950 Sugar Bowl, an LSU player created controversy during game week by _____.

a. robbing a New Orleans bank
b. spying on Oklahoma practices
c. stealing the Sooner Schooner
d. trying to change teams

134. During the January 1, 1963, Orange Bowl, the Sooners were visited in the locker room by whom?

a. Bear Bryant
b. John F. Kennedy
c. Jimi Hendrix
d. Neil Armstrong

135. Four Oklahoma players were ruled ineligible on the eve of the 1965 Gator Bowl for what reason?

a. they had broken curfew
b. they had raided Florida State's team hotel
c. they had signed professional contracts
d. they had been playing as seventh-year seniors

136. Oklahoma edged Florida State 18–17 in the 1981 Orange Bowl thanks to what scoring play on the Sooners' final possession?

a. a field goal
b. an interception return
c. a safety
d. a two-point conversion

137. During the 1985 Orange Bowl loss to Washington, the Sooners were penalized 15 yards and three points because of what infraction?

a. Oklahoma's offense played the entire first quarter with 12 players on the field.
b. The Sooner Schooner ran onto the field after an Oklahoma field goal without permission.
c. Oklahoma's cheerleaders accidentally entered the field of play while the clock was still running.
d. Coach Barry Switzer remained on the sidelines after being ejected in the fourth quarter.

138. Oklahoma missed out on another national title with a 20–14 loss to which team in the 1988 Orange Bowl?

a. Michigan
b. Florida
c. Florida State
d. Miami

139. Clemson's 13–6 victory over Oklahoma in the 1989 Citrus Bowl represented the ACC's first win against Oklahoma in how many attempts?

a. 9
b. 16
c. 28
d. 32

140. What now-defunct bowl game did Oklahoma play in 1994?

a. the Pewter Bowl
b. the Copper Bowl
c. the Iron Bowl
d. the Steel Bowl

MEMORABLE PLAYERS

141. As of the 2008 season, how many Sooners have been the runner-up to the Heisman Trophy?

   a. 3
   b. 5
   c. 7
   d. 9

142. Which player has NOT been an Outland Trophy winner? The award is given to the game's most outstanding interior lineman.

   a. Jammal Brown
   b. Greg Roberts
   c. Ryan Fisher
   d. Lee Roy Selman

143. Center Tom Brahaney in 2007 became the _____ Oklahoma player inducted into the College Football Hall of Fame.

   a. 7th
   b. 12th
   c. 18th
   d. 25th

144. In a 2001 game against Kansas, Trent Smith set a Sooner record for most touchdown receptions in a single game with how many?

   a. 3
   b. 4
   c. 5
   d. 6

145. From 1976 to 1978, kicker Uwe von Schamann converted how many consecutive extra points in his career for a Sooner record?

a. 81
b. 115
c. 140
d. 201

146. Who holds the Oklahoma record, going into the 2008 season, for both tackles in a single game (23) and single season (189)?

a. Jackie Shipp
b. Daryl Hunt
c. Kevin Murphy
d. Rick Bryan

147. Which Sooner set a school record with five sacks in a 1994 game against Texas Tech?

a. Martin Chase
b. Cedric Jones
c. Kelly Gregg
d. Rodney Rideau

148. Which rapper derived his stage name from an All-American receiver at Oklahoma?

a. Snoop Dogg
b. Busta Rhymes
c. Sean Combs
d. Common

149. That player is in the Oklahoma record books for _____.

a. returning a kickoff 100 yards for a touchdown
b. receiving five touchdown passes in a single game
c. having five 200-yard receiving games in his career
d. starting 32 consecutive games

150. **In 1973, Tony DiRienzo kicked what became Oklahoma's longest field goal. How long was it?**
    a. 69 yards
    b. 60 yards
    c. 57 yards
    d. 52 yards

151. **Which player tied a school record with a 96-yard rushing touchdown against North Texas in 1995?**
    a. James Allen
    b. De'Mond Parker
    c. Jerald Moore
    d. Jeff Frazier

152. **Which freshman in 1945 returned an interception the entire length of the field for a touchdown against Kansas State?**
    a. Al Needs
    b. Joe Golding
    c. Johnny West
    d. Hugh Ballard

153. **Entering the 2008 season, who holds Oklahoma's receiving records for receptions (221), yards (3,241), and touchdowns (31) in a career?**
    a. Quentin Griffin
    b. Trent Smith
    c. Mark Clayton
    d. Malcolm Kelly

154. **How many 100-yard receiving games did Mark Clayton have in his career for an Oklahoma record?**
    a. 10
    b. 15
    c. 20
    d. 25

155. Oklahoma's career points leader, going into the 2008 season, is _____.

a. running back Steve Owens
b. kicker R.D. Lashar
c. kicker Tim Lashar
d. running back Billy Sims

156. Oklahoma produced three brothers who were all All-Americans. Who were they?

a. Steve, Tinker, and Dave Owens
b. Buddy, Bill, and Kurt Burris
c. Lee Roy, Dewey, and Lucious Selmon
d. Tommy, John, and Kevin McDonald

157. Which player was a three-time All-American?

a. Rod Shoate
b. Brian Bosworth
c. Anthony Phillips
d. Jammal Brown

158. Which Oklahoma player, who scored on a 61-yard touchdown run, was named offensive MVP of the 1980 Orange Bowl against Florida State?

a. quarterback J.C. Watts
b. halfback Billy Sims
c. fullback Stanley Wilson
d. tight end Forrest Valora

159. Which Oklahoma kicker converted four field goals during the Sooners' 25–10 victory over Penn State in the 1986 Orange Bowl?

a. Mike Keeling
b. Tim Lashar
c. R.D. Lashar
d. Tim Duncan

160. **Billy Sims set a Big Eight single-season rushing record in 1978 with how many yards?**

    a. 952
    b. 1,220
    c. 1,466
    d. 1,896

161. **How many yards per carry did Sims average that year, when he led the nation in rushing?**

    a. 3
    b. 5
    c. 7
    d. 9

162. **How many 200-yard rushing games did Billy Sims rack up during the 1978 season?**

    a. 2
    b. 4
    c. 5
    d. 7

163. **What was Billy Vessels's nickname?**

    a. "curly"
    b. "skinny"
    c. "speedy"
    d. "burly"

164. **How many touchdowns did Billy Vessels score during his senior season in 1952, the year he won the Heisman Trophy?**

    a. 10
    b. 12
    c. 17
    d. 20

165. Vessels was a first-round draft pick of Baltimore Colts in 1953 but opted instead to play for which team?

a. the Edmonton Eskimos
b. the Chicago Bears
c. the Brooklyn Dodgers
d. the Chicago Cardinals

166. Entering the 2008 season, who is Oklahoma's all-time leading scorer with 57 career touchdowns?

a. Steve Owens
b. Tommy McDonald
c. Adrian Peterson
d. Jason White

167. What was Oklahoma's record the season Steve Owens won the Heisman Trophy?

a. 10–0
b. 9–1
c. 8–2
d. 6–4

168. Steve Owens set a Sooner record with how many carries in a single game?

a. 35
b. 45
c. 55
d. 65

IN THE PROS

169. Which former Sooner was named the NFL's Rookie of the Year in 2007?

   a. Adrian Peterson
   b. Davin Joseph
   c. Mark Clayton
   d. Marshawn Lynch

170. He was drafted by and played for what team?

   a. the Chicago Bears
   b. the Green Bay Packers
   c. the Detroit Lions
   d. the Minnesota Vikings

171. Which Sooner tight end has gone on to more than a decade-long career in the NFL and was named a Pro Bowler with the Washington Redskins?

   a. Trent Smith
   b. Stephen Alexander
   c. Adrian Cooper
   d. Joey Mickey

172. In what round was Josh Heupel drafted in 2001?

   a. 1st
   b. 2nd
   c. 6th
   d. he wasn't drafted

173. Which All-American halfback from the 1950s was elected as a receiver to the Pro Football Hall of Fame in 1998?

   a. Tommy McDonald
   b. Clendon Thomas
   c. Greg Pruitt
   d. Steve Owens

174. Which former Sooner was the first Detroit Lion to ever gain more than 1,000 yards in a season?

   a. Billy Sims
   b. Steve Owens
   c. Leon Crosswhite
   d. John Flynn

175. Who has been Oklahoma's only offensive player selected with the No. 1 overall pick in the NFL draft?

   a. Adrian Peterson
   b. Billy Sims
   c. Steve Zabel
   d. Dave Baker

176. Who has been their only defensive player selected as No. 1?

   a. Roy Williams
   b. Cedric Jones
   c. Lee Roy Selmon
   d. Carl McAdams

177. Who was NOT one of Oklahoma's three first-round draft picks in 1976?

   a. Lee Roy Selmon
   b. Dewey Selmon
   c. Joe Washington
   d. Billy Brooks

178. Which NFL team, going into the 2008 draft, has historically chosen the most Sooners?

a. the Arizona/St. Louis Cardinals
b. the Chicago Bears
c. the St. Louis/Los Angeles Rams
d. the Green Bay Packers

179. The most Sooners ever taken in a single draft was in 1988. How many were there?

a. 8
b. 10
c. 13
d. 16

COACHES

180. Who was NOT an early Oklahoma head coach?
- a. Fred Roberts
- b. Fred Ewing
- c. Bennie Owen
- d. Owen Rich

181. Which Oklahoma coach is NOT in the College Football Hall of Fame?
- a. Barry Switzer
- b. Bud Wilkinson
- c. Bennie Owen
- d. Tom Stidham

182. Who replaced Barry Switzer as head coach in 1989?
- a. Howard Schnellenberger
- b. Gary Gibbs
- c. John Blake
- d. Chuck Fairbanks

183. Which Sooner coach's career was cut short when he died of a heart attack after only one season?
- a. Chuck Fairbanks
- b. Jim Mackenzie
- c. Jim Tatum
- d. Lawrence Jones

184. Which former national championship-winning coach at Miami lasted one season at Oklahoma?
- a. Dennis Erickson
- b. Jimmy Johnson
- c. Butch Davis
- d. Howard Schnellenberger

STREAKS AND RECORDS

185. Oklahoma holds the longest winning streak in Div. I history with _____ consecutive games.

   a. 26
   b. 32
   c. 39
   d. 47

186. Which team snapped that streak in 1957?

   a. Alabama
   b. Michigan
   c. Ohio State
   d. Notre Dame

187. Oklahoma leads the nation, going into the 2008 season, with the most all-time _____.

   a. All-Americans
   b. points scored
   c. victories
   d. Heisman Trophy winners

188. Which Oklahoma team set an NCAA record averaging 427 yards of offense per game?

a. the 2000 team
b. the 1985 team
c. the 1975 team
d. the 1971 team

189. The 1993 Oklahoma State team, the 1946 Texas A&M team, and the 1938 Washington State team all hold what dubious distinction against the Sooners?

a. They lost twice to Oklahoma in a single season.
b. They were held to a single first down.
c. They amassed zero yards of total offense.
d. They gave up 70 points to the Sooners.

190. What are the most times Oklahoma, historically known for its ground game, has ever rushed the ball in a single game? The record dates back to 1972, when the Sooners averaged 86.8 plays per game.

a. 49
b. 65
c. 88
d. 101

191. The 1975 team produced the most Oklahoma All-Americans in a single season. How many were there?

a. 5
b. 7
c. 9
d. 11

192. From 1971 to 1988, Oklahoma had a stretch of 18 consecutive seasons with _____.

a. at least 10 wins
b. a Heisman Trophy finalist
c. a New Year's bowl invite
d. at least one All-American

193. What were the most points Oklahoma has ever scored in a single game?

a. 70
b. 82
c. 94
d. 110

194. In that game, how many rushing touchdowns did the Sooners score?

a. 6
b. 8
c. 10
d. 12

195. How many points per game did the 1956 offense average?

a. 35.5
b. 40
c. 46.6
d. 52.2

196. In the 2006 matchup with Nebraska, how many sacks did the Sooners make to tie a school record?

a. 4
b. 6
c. 8
d. 9

197. The Oklahoma defense has recorded more than _____ shutouts in the program's history.

   a. 50
   b. 100
   c. 200
   d. 250

198. Oklahoma has won more games than any program in college football since _____.

   a. the team's inception
   b. the NCAA began keeping records
   c. World War II
   d. 1970

199. Oklahoma has spent more time _____ than any other program.

   a. in the top-25 rankings
   b. the AP top-5 rankings
   c. at No. 1
   d. defending national championships

200. Oklahoma won 102 games in what decade?

   a. 1950s
   b. 1960s
   c. 1970s
   d. 1980s

ANSWERS

1. b)	22. b)	43. c)	64. a)
2. d)	23. a)	44. c)	65. d)
3. c)	24. d)	45. b)	66. b)
4. b)	25. d)	46. c)	67. d)
5. c)	26. c)	47. b)	68. c)
6. b)	27. b)	48. d)	69. d)
7. c)	28. b)	49. a)	70. a)
8. d)	29. a)	50. b)	71. c)
9. a)	30. c)	51. d)	72. c)
10. d)	31. a)	52. b)	73. a)
11. b)	32. d)	53. b)	74. b)
12. d)	33. d)	54. d)	75. b)
13. b)	34. d)	55. b)	76. b)
14. c)	35. c)	56. d)	77. b)
15. d)	36. c)	57. c)	78. a)
16. d)	37. b)	58. d)	79. a)
17. d)	38. a)	59. a)	80. c)
18. c)	39. c)	60. b)	81. d)
19. a)	40. d)	61. b)	82. c)
20. b)	41. c)	62. b)	83. b)
21. c)	42. b)	63. d)	84. b)

85. b)	114. d)	143. c)	172. c)
86. a)	115. b)	144. b)	173. a)
87. c)	116. c)	145. c)	174. b)
88. a)	117. c)	146. a)	175. b)
89. d)	118. c)	147. b)	176. c)
90. b)	119. d)	148. b)	177. b)
91. a)	120. c)	149. a)	178. a)
92. b)	121. d)	150. b)	179. c)
93. a)	122. d)	151. d)	180. d)
94. b)	123. d)	152. a)	181. d)
95. b)	124. a)	153. c)	182. b)
96. b)	125. d)	154. b)	183. b)
97. c)	126. b)	155. a)	184. d)
98. d)	127. b)	156. c)	185. d)
99. b)	128. b)	157. a)	186. d)
100. a)	129. a)	158. a)	187. b)
101. c)	130. a)	159. b)	188. d)
102. c)	131. a)	160. d)	189. b)
103. b)	132. b)	161. c)	190. c)
104. c)	133. b)	162. b)	191. c)
105. a)	134. b)	163. a)	192. d)
106. d)	135. c)	164. c)	193. b)
107. b)	136. d)	165. a)	194. d)
108. c)	137. b)	166. a)	195. c)
109. a)	138. d)	167. d)	196. d)
110. a)	139. b)	168. c)	197. d)
111. c)	140. b)	169. a)	198. c)
112. d)	141. b)	170. d)	199. b)
113. b)	142. c)	171. b)	200. c)